S0-DZG-793

Headline Series

No. 274   **FOREIGN POLICY ASSOCIATION** $4.00

AUTHENTIC DEVELOPMENT IN AFRICA

by Brian W. Walker

Foreword

Cover by Hersch Wartik;
photo of village south of Agadez, Niger, by Mark Edwards/Earthscan

The Author

BRIAN W. WALKER was director-general of
Oxfam, Britain's largest private voluntary devel-
opment and relief organization, from 1974–83.
From 1983–85 he was director of the Independent
Commission on International Humanitarian
Issues in Geneva. In 1985 he was appointed
president of the International Institute for Envi-
ronment and Development based in Washington,
London and Buenos Aires. He has traveled widely
in the Third World, especially in Africa.

The Foreign Policy Association

The Foreign Policy Association is a private, nonprofit, nonpartisan educational
organization. Its purpose is to stimulate wider interest and more effective
participation in, and greater understanding of, world affairs among American
citizens. Among its activities is the continuous publication, dating from 1935, of
the HEADLINE SERIES. The author is responsible for factual accuracy and for the
views expressed. FPA itself takes no position on issues of United States foreign
policy.

HEADLINE SERIES (ISSN 0017-8780) is published five times a year, January, March,
May, September and November, by the Foreign Policy Association, Inc., 205
Lexington Ave., New York, N.Y. 10016. Chairman, Leonard H. Marks; President,
Archie E. Albright; Editor, Nancy L. Hoepli; Senior Editor, Ann R. Monjo; Associate
Editor, K. M. Rohan. Subscription rates, $15.00 for 5 issues; $25.00 for 10 issues;
$30.00 for 15 issues. Single copy price $4.00. Discount 25% on 10 to 99 copies; 30% on
100 to 499; 35% on 500 to 999; 40% on 1,000 or more. Payment must accompany order
for $8 or less. Add $1 for postage. Second-class postage paid at New York, N.Y.
POSTMASTER: Send address changes to HEADLINE SERIES, Foreign Policy Association, 205 Lexington Ave., New York, N.Y. 10016. Copyright 1985 by Foreign Policy
Association, Inc. Composed and printed at Science Press, Ephrata, Pa.

Library of Congress Catalog Card No. 85-82567
ISBN 0-87124-102-1

Foreword

" Authentic Development in Africa" is a welcome contribution to the small but growing number of studies of the current crisis in Africa. At a time when both Asia and Latin America are showing signs of sustained economic development, relative political stability, increased food production per capita and lower fertility rates, Africa's vital signs are pointed in the wrong direction. Throughout most of that troubled continent, per capita incomes and food production have declined for over a decade while birthrates are the highest in the world and still rising.

These long-term trends were accelerated by the severe drought affecting Ethiopia, Sudan and much of the Sahel, as well as Angola, Botswana and Mozambique, during 1984–85. The resulting crisis led to the starvation of thousands of Africans and placed millions of others in conditions of a most precarious poverty, removed from their land, far from their homes, dependent upon food aid for survival. The role of world public opinion, mobilized by the power of television and by aggressive fundraising campaigns by many agencies, helped to generate funds from governments and private contributions in unprecedented amounts, and helped to save the lives of millions of people who might otherwise have died. The media, the musicians, the major relief and development agencies and the newly formed United Nations Office for Emergency Operations in Africa can take pride in the remarkable accomplishment of generating and distributing food and other assistance so quickly during 1985, thus averting a catastrophe of major proportions.

But the achievements of the international relief efforts, and the improved rains over much of the continent in 1985, do not mean that the problems have been solved. In most cases, the underlying causes of the emergency are as serious as ever and the need for a better understanding of the long-term problems and identification of practical solutions is urgent.

In late 1985 the United Nations Children's Fund published a report pleading for more attention to the human dimension of the current crisis, *Within Human Reach: A Future for Africa's Children*. Brian W. Walker and UNICEF share a common orientation: the long-term solutions to Africa's problems must be found by Africans themselves. Outside funds and assistance are needed, but they must build upon authentic African cultures and institutions and utilize Africa's greatest resource, its people. Appropriate development must build on traditional technologies and recognize the central role played by women. In particular, aid programs must focus on the small-farm sector, and shift the planning and support processes from short-term "projects" to long-term strategies.

Mr. Walker notes four central points that deserve our attention:

1. *Poverty is the real problem,* and must be addressed as such. Famine and drought are merely symptoms.

2. *Basic human needs must be met* before Africans can be in a position to achieve other goals.

3. *Agriculture must return to the basics,* making small farmers and herders self-sufficient before trying to tackle large-scale, capital-intensive and energy-intensive forms of production.

4. *Aid must be directed to the rural poor.*

Many have paid lip service to such objectives for many years, but Brian Walker's study helps to point the way to achieving these goals by mobilizing the energies of African people themselves. People-focused approaches have already been proving themselves, even in the current difficult circumstances. Over the past year, small farmers in Zimbabwe produced a bumper

4

national harvest as a result of the government's recognizing and relying on their contribution. In Burkina Faso, immunization against measles, meningitis and yellow fever was increased to nearly 70 percent coverage of young children in a few months after the government turned to the people to help. Even in the disastrous conditions of drought and famine, evidence from many nongovernmental organizations and international agencies has proved the potential of people to respond once they are given a role and some resources to play their own creative part in the relief and rehabilitation process. We have seen the beginnings of a Child Survival and Development Revolution, even in the midst of drought and disaster. But it will depend on people to carry it through.

Those of us involved with Africa from the outside have our own part to play in support of African initiatives, particularly in ways which encourage the human-focused approaches set forth in this book. I would particularly stress that those involved in economic policy, bankers and international financial agencies included, have their part to play by supporting these people-focused initiatives through "adjustment policy with a human face."

Ultimately, as in any continent or any country, Africa's future must be built by Africans themselves. The job for the rest of us is to help them as we can, and, especially, not to make the task even more difficult than it already is.

James P. Grant

January 1986

Mr. Grant is the executive director of UNICEF. A former assistant administrator of the U.S. Agency for International Development, Mr. Grant was president of the Overseas Development Council in Washington before joining UNICEF in 1980.

5

AREAS MOST CRITICALLY AFFECTED BY THE DROUGHT

As of June 1985

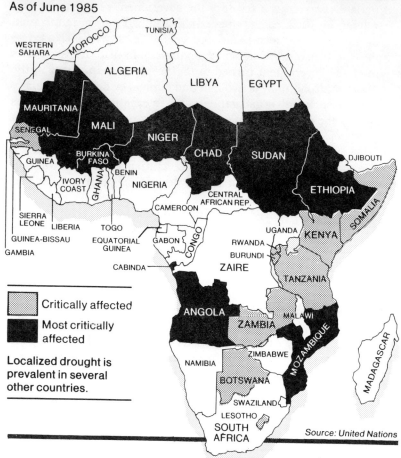

Critically affected

Most critically affected

Localized drought is prevalent in several other countries.

Source: United Nations

The Horn of Africa includes Sudan, Ethiopia, Djibouti, Somalia and Kenya.

The Sahel (meaning desert's edge) includes Mauritania, Senegal, The Gambia, Burkina Faso, Mali, Niger and Chad.

1

Africa Today
and
Tomorrow

Twenty years have passed since Julius K. Nyerere, until recently president of Tanzania and chairman of the Organization of African Unity (OAU), advised the world that "Africa is in a mess." Today, 101 years after the Conference of Berlin, Africa is in a worse and accelerating "mess."

It is easy to analyze Africa's problems, rather more difficult to propose solutions. German Chancellor Otto von Bismarck stage-managed the Conference of Berlin in 1884–85 which shaped Africa as it is known today. Explorer Henry Stanley recognized the conference for what it was: a scramble by the Europeans for new territory and the prospect of cheap food, mineral wealth and new markets. He compared Europe's rapaciousness to the way in which his "black followers used to rush with gleaming knives for slaughtered game during our travels." He was right. The contemporary political map of Africa reflects the boundary lines drawn in Berlin over 100 years ago. Over 1,000 cultural groups have been forced into some 50 "sovereign" nations, with scant regard for the natural resources of the land, the cultural mores of the people, their 2,000 different languages or their many religions. Although Africans, especially since World War II, have increasingly ignored those sovereign boundaries in their local trade and travel, the political divisions continue to exert a detrimental influence on millions of people.

The major cost of colonialism, for which Africans are paying today, was the breakdown of pastoralism, nomadism and settled living. Pastoralists raise livestock for their subsistence. Nomads are roving pastoralists. Hitherto, people had carefully constructed a balance with their environment. This balance was the key not merely to survival, but to food abundance and the evolution of rich civilizations over three millennia.

Africa, the cradle of the human experiment, has fossilized remains going back 5 million years, and there is evidence suggesting human form as long as 10 million years ago. Africa has demanded from the human species a respect for its biological carrying systems—the plants and animals that its land and water will support without suffering degradation—and its climatic features as the condition for survival. Wisely, people accepted that condition and organized their patterns of life to accommodate increasing drought in the north, accelerating wetness in the equatorial regions, fragile soils throughout most of the continent, arid zones with lakes and rivers appearing and disappearing and, throughout, a rich diversity of flora and fauna, even in the drier parts of the continent.

Shifting patterns of living, with barter as the medium of exchange between tribes, were the norm. Where nature precluded settled life, complex and highly effective forms of nomadism ensured not only the safety but the rich fulfillment of community life. Tribal records reaching back 3,000 years reveal that people did die in extremes of drought or flood, but, population growth notwithstanding, there was nothing remotely comparable to the scale of human death and suffering experienced today as a result of poverty-induced hunger and malnutrition. In fact, one of the striking features of precolonial Africa was the diversity and volume of food produced. This was often commented upon by

18th- and 19th-century explorers, who noted the variety of foods and the custom of holding three years' harvests in reserve. Nikolai Ivanovich Vavilov, the Russian botanist who tried to trace the origins of various plants by locating areas with the greatest number and diversity of their species, on visiting Ethiopia in the mid-1930s was amazed at the genetic diversity in that now barren land. What today is southern Mali, drought-stricken and famine-ridden, was once known as the breadbasket of Africa. To the north, on the borders of the Sahara Desert, land was carefully husbanded and could be left fallow for two decades; those who cultivated the soil offered the nomads land for pasture in the dry season and grain in exchange for milk, manure for the fields and donkeys for plowing.

For centuries the world has taken from Africa but put little back. From the 16th century onward, 20 million slaves were brought to the Americas. Another 10 million died before embarkation or during passage. Hundreds of thousands of others were moved eastward into the Arab world and Asia. In one sense, colonialism built on this pattern of exploitation, substituting land, crop and mineral wealth for the human resources. Colonialism put a stop to pastoralism and nomadism. It abolished the economics of barter, but offered little in its place other than the political and legal framework of the market economy. Local wealth, the essential dynamic of a market economy, was not stimulated. If people do not have money in their pockets to fuel it, the market economy cannot work.

Nature cannot carry, or sustain, large settled populations if the soil is inadequate to support them or if the water supply is so erratic as to prohibit monoculture (single-plant crops)—the dominant agricultural system introduced by the colonials. It is less than 100 years since the British first hoisted the Union Jack over Salisbury, in the territory claimed by Cecil Rhodes. Today Salisbury is an attractive city with over three quarters of a million inhabitants. But neither the change of its name to Harare and that of Rhodesia to Zimbabwe nor the change of the administration from British to Zimbabwean has increased one jot the carrying capacity of the environment.

Postindependence Africa

The ending of colonialism left most independent territories woefully inadequate to compete in the post-1945 world. At independence, Mozambique, for example, had two doctors and a dozen typists; the Belgian Congo (now Zaire), 13 college graduates. Independence opened the way to two additional trends, both of which are integral to the horrendous suffering of 1986.

On the one hand, there has been the moral failure of African political leadership. With few exceptions, greed, corruption and the sheer inability to cope have dominated the middle and upper echelons in much of independent Africa. When this poverty of leadership is compounded by inadequate bureaucracies, ill-disciplined armies, an all-too-fragile economic base and a collapsing ecosystem, there is an obvious recipe for human tragedy on a huge scale. When those "local" conditions are set within a world framework in which political and trade power is significantly biased in favor of the North, that is, the more economically developed, industrialized countries, and against African interests, then cynicism begins to pervade the process of decisionmaking.

On the other hand, the development model promoted by donor countries and their agencies has failed. Arguably, the most basic responsibility of any government is that of producing food or buying food to feed its people. Many African countries, such as the Sudan, have chosen, in fact, to seek food security by basing agricultural policies on the dominant, high-energy, "high tech" model developed in the North, with its emphasis on output per farmer instead of output per unit of land, its insatiable demand for costly inputs, its reliance on monocropping and nonfood cash crops and its allocation of power to those who are not dependent on the soil, whether African or non-African.

Once President Richard M. Nixon and his successors embraced the ideology of the Williams Report of 1971, *United States International Economic Policy in an Interdependent World* (see Reading List on p. 68), which recommended that U.S. foreign policy and U.S. trade should benefit from U.S. foreign aid policies, the die was cast against African interests, and risk capital was at a premium. This is not a moral judgment but a factual one.

Sudanese winnow sun-dried beans on an island in the Nile.

The judgment applies, with isolated exceptions that include the 1985 public response throughout the North, to European and Japanese aid as well. Once aid becomes a prime tool of foreign policy and economic power and loses its humanitarian motivation, its integrity is in question.

This is not to say that sovereign governments do not have the right to benefit from "aid." They do, and in democracies, governments that do not seek benefits may not be reelected. It is, however, morally repugnant to dress up aid that clearly, patently and explicitly benefits the donor substantially, and the recipient marginally, as an act of humanity. It is nothing of the sort, and to pretend otherwise is humbug.

Reverse Aid

For instance, the South over many years has supplied germ plasm, which is essential to plant breeding, to the United States. The value of this steady transfer is immense. Consider one simple example. The stalk of a wild variety of tomato (*L. Cheesmanii*

11

146) has made it possible for plant breeders to grow fruit that can be harvested mechanically. This has contributed immeasurably to the development of the U.S. tomato-growing industry with incalculable consequences for the canning, bottling and soft-drink industries and for the nation's health. That example alone, not to mention similar genetic contributions to cereals, vegetables, fruit trees or animal stock that add to America's food security, should give pause for thought.

Northern aid policies toward Africa must undergo considerable evolution before Africa makes advances in food security similar to those achieved in parts of Southeast Asia or India's Punjab.

In terms of aid, the Soviet Union and the People's Republic of China have not contributed anything of real value to the people of Africa either. Soviet aid, parsimonious in the extreme, is mainly in the form of weapons, military training, ideological models and political interference. Chinese aid in the days of Chairman Mao Zedong was limited principally to the building of a railway in Tanzania. The aid from both countries has offered an ideological model for development, in contrast to other models that stress high technology, the transfer of management skills or small-scale "people" development.

Three Positive Trends

If North American, European, Soviet and Chinese aid to Africa has, in the aggregate, done little to help the continent, then what should be done now? The short- to medium-term outlook remains bleak. There are, however, trends that inspire confidence in the long-term future.

First, some African leaders are now giving evidence of beginning to come to grips with the challenge of poverty and environmental bankruptcy. This appears to be the case in Niger and Burkina Faso (formerly Upper Volta) and provides a glimmer of hope for change.

Second, despite the above-mentioned strictures about the integrity of Northern aid, it remains a fact that the assistance programs of the U.S. Agency for International Development (AID), private voluntary organizations like the American Friends Service Committee, CARE and the Oxford Committee for Famine Relief (Oxfam), and United Nations agencies like the UN Children's Fund (UNICEF), the World Health Organization (WHO) and the UN Development Program (UNDP) offer excellent examples of what can be done to help Africa stave off a daunting future. These aid success stories need to be identified and painstakingly analyzed. Once this is done, these programs need to be replicated across Africa. And while time is desperately short, it has not run out altogether.

Third, there lies within the African people not only immense patience but a buoyancy and generosity of spirit that is worthy of emulation around the world. Perhaps because of their capacity to work with nature, to live within the interstices of a volatile climate, to harmonize community living with the demanding and difficult conditions of their environment and to laugh in the face of adversity, Africans are survivors first and foremost. Those human qualities, lying deep within the African character, forged out of thousands of years of experience, provide a stable and immensely powerful foundation on which to rebuild Africa. Africa's hope lies essentially with the African people. The rural poor are an asset, not a liability. With modest support from the outside, they have the capacity to rebuild their great continent. As to the future, Pliny the Elder (A.D. 23-79) observed, "Out of Africa there is always something new." That potential remains.

2

When 'Milk Comes Frozen
Home in Pail'

Shakespeare's words record the problems encountered by milk-maids in 16th-century Britain. The playwright was unaware that he lived at the peak of the "little ice age" that dominated northern Europe between 1450 and 1850. Nevertheless, he had to do battle with the cold and the snow each long winter. Ten years ago, a British meteorologist, Derek Winstanley, who now works as an atmospheric scientist at the Brookhaven National Laboratory on Long Island, N.Y., advised that the drought conditions dominating much of sub-Saharan Africa might be related to the frequency, or infrequency, of severe winters in Britain. He suggested that the westerly winds that determine much of Britain's climate also play a significant part in changes taking place in Africa. What is happening, Winstanley argued, is part of a long-term trend, not just a passing aberration after which "normal" weather will return. (Normal weather is defined as the 30-year mean value for the period 1941–70.) If the drought of 1968–73 was simply the result of a random variable in rainfall, then 6 consecutive years without rain might occur once in every 64 years. But the drought has lasted, with a brief reprieve in

1974, for 17 years, and the odds against that are 1 to 125,000. Another 3 years of drought would lengthen those odds to 1 in a million.

Has the mean itself declined? By analyzing 130 years of records, including those kept meticulously by early explorers like Mungo Park and Wilhelm Junker for the Sahelian drought zone and the Horn of Africa, Winstanley can show that seasonal rainfall—June to September—has been steadily and consistently declining for more than two centuries. In the last 10 years, it has been 20 percent below normal. That decline is reflected also in the discharges of rivers in the same region.

Despite this long-term trend in the weather, fluctuations can still occur in odd years when so-called normal rainfall encourages people, governments and donor agencies to believe that "the bad spell has broken." Such a year was 1974. But a fluctuation of this kind does not reverse the trend; it merely relieves the pressure for 12 months.

The 1985 rains led the UN's Food and Agriculture Organization (FAO) and others to advise that the drought had ended, the rains had returned and food aid would not be required in many countries which had needed it in 1984–85. But already it is clear that this is not the case. By the fall of 1985, Zimbabwe, despite excellent harvests that year, was experiencing rain shortages leading to seed-germination failure. In the Sudan, the so-called rains were far too patchy to give any real confidence as to the future. Field workers predict a 1986 famine as bad as 1985, with 5 million people at risk. It must be assumed that in the Sahel the rule is increasing drought, and the exception, rain. Sahelian development policies increasingly will have to reflect that reality.

The Sahara's Lake Oyo

Development strategists working in the Sahel and the Horn of Africa will probably have to base their future planning on shifts in the weather measured in geological time rather than contemporary history. By studying lake levels over the last 30,000 years, for example, wet and dry trends can be identified. The driest part of the Sahara was once a substantial lake. An oval region running southeast from Libya to southern Egypt and northern Sudan—the Oyo depression—gives evidence of buried mud flats with algal remains, charcoal and pollen. Lake Oyo, replenished by fresh water, was surrounded by tropical savanna woodland between 7000 and 3000 B.C. John Gribbin, author of *Future Weather*, notes that since the dynastic Egypt of the pharaohs (3100 B.C.) began at this time, it is conceivable that the ancient Egyptians were driven north to the flood plains of the Nile by the drying out of the desert.

Meanwhile, 800 miles to the southeast of the Oyo depression, at Lake Chad in Mali, French researchers have found evidence of shells, plants and animal remains, and malarial swamp conditions as well as human tombs, which they date at 7500–4000 B.C. and again, after a dry period, at 3000–2000 B.C.

Dr. Vance Haynes of the University of Arizona, who uncovered the Lake Oyo evidence with colleagues from Toronto University, says there is evidence of another rainfall lake north of Oyo, which existed 10,000 years ago when Oyo was dry. Dr. Haynes concludes, not unreasonably, that the Sahara is meteorologically unstable and that "the rain has been switching from nothing to 12-16 inches many times over geological periods." He adds that the present Sahel disaster "looks like a minor variation on a much bigger cycle" and that "the key question is: Are we seeing a new trend? Is the Sahel moving south?"

Certainly, for the last 8,000 years the Sahara has been getting progressively drier. From Senegal to Ethiopia the rains in 1984 were about half the average, causing the worst drought year on record. The Nile flood in 1984 was the lowest in 350 years; that important watershed has been shrinking for at least 5 years. The Niger river, which runs through the capital city of Niamey, has virtually dried out for the first time in this century. (The Blue Nile draws its headwaters from Ethiopia; the Niger, from Mali and Guinea.) Lake Chad has also dried out and is only a tenth the size it was in the 1950s and 1960s. Indeed, in northeast Nigeria it has receded so far from one of its feeder canals that no winter crop of wheat has been planted. People are trying to live on the former lake floor and to farm the mud flats.

Professor Emeritus Herbert Lamb of the Climatic Research Unit, University of East Anglia, Norwich, England, noted in a letter to the London *Times* that "one analysis of the rainfalls measured in the Sahel zone since the beginning of this century hinted at a roughly 200-year-long cycle (with its latest peak around the 1930s) which may correspond with a better-known indicator of a fluctuation of about that length in the sun." Given a 200-year-long trend, a variable lasting 5 or even 10 years would still be a variable and not a reversal in the trend. In its latest study, the Climatic Research Unit in Norwich has extended the reliable record of Northern Hemispheric temperature fluctuations back to 1851, showing that the world has been warming up since then, with only minor variations. There was a sudden spurt of warming in the 1970s, just as the African droughts and North American winters intensified.

By reconstructing other records relating to equatorial Africa, Winstanley can show some evidence of an opposite trend there of increased rainfall levels, thus demonstrating the instability of climate over the landmass as a whole.

Climate and Man

That all these conditions are interrelated can be better substantiated now than when Winstanley first presented his evidence. Climate, says Winstanley, is the key to drought in the Sahel and the Horn of Africa, as well as to the opposite trend further south, in Equatorial Africa. Both trends are rooted in climatic changes that predate Homo sapiens, he says. "Human pressure on the land and degradation of the vegetation cover can be expected to produce changes in the energy and hydrological cycles. . . . However, there is no scientific consensus as to the sensitivity and response of climates to these man-made modifications to the ground cover. I see no good reason why degradation of the surface environment by man should cause rainfall to decrease in the sub-Sahara zone and increase in parts of East Africa," he wrote in a recent article in *Weatherwise*.

Three more years of drought and all the suffering involved is a high price to pay before policymakers are forced to alter their

The Trend of Mean Annual Rainfall:
Sub-Saharan Africa

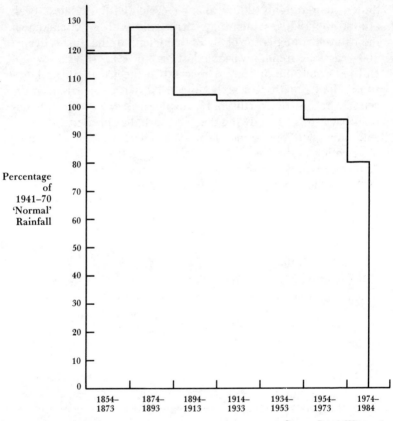

Source: Derek Winstanley

This graph is based on data combined for many locations in a manner that gives equal emphasis to relative changes at each of them. The graph shows successive 20-year averages of rainfall as a percent of the 1941–70 "normal" rainfall. The bottom of the graph is deliberately extended to zero percent to put the large magnitude of the decline in rainfall in perspective.

18

The Trend of Mean Annual Rainfall:
Parts of Equatorial Africa

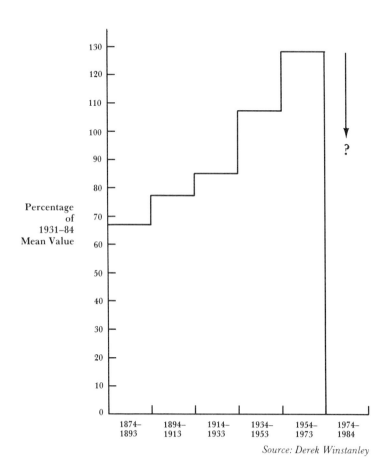

Source: Derek Winstanley

The data for this graph has been derived in a manner that gives equal emphasis to relative changes at each of many locations in the zone. The net increase in rainfall in this zone is seen to aggregate to nearly a doubling since the 19th century.

development strategies in order to take long-term account of continuing and deepening drought conditions from Senegal and Mauritania in the west to Somalia and Ethiopia in the east. The possibility that global climatic changes are not cyclical but follow a linear progression and that in North Africa climate aggravated by human folly is the dominant influence on development must be accepted.

Famine Prediction

Part of the equipment to cope with longer-term trends lies with early-warning systems aimed at famine prediction. There are two tools currently available, the FAO's early-warning system and satellite technology. While better than nothing, they are inadequate for this purpose. The FAO's early-warning system, which uses estimates of rainfall, population and food production, is handicapped by problems ranging from overstretched and inexperienced bureaucracies, sometimes operating in civil-war conditions, to the deliberate manipulation of figures so as to attract greater budgetary support to national treasuries. Despite every effort to overcome these problems, the estimates lack scientific accuracy, but at least they provide useful warning signals. (It is worth noting that the Ethiopian Relief and Rehabilitation Commission has warned the donor community of a mounting food crisis each year since the mid-1970s. Their warnings, however, have been largely ignored.)

Satellite technology, while much improved in recent years, is still not the tool disaster-response agencies would wish it to be. Satellites can monitor general vegetative conditions, but, as Peter Cutler notes in a recent issue of the journal *Disasters*, "Unfortunately, these indicators are often extremely rudimentary and can only give a very broad guide to regions which are likely to face problems, rather than the actual population groups likely to be affected. Neither can rainfall and crop monitoring, even where substantially accurate, tell us very much about when people are likely to be forced to move away from their homes. . . ."

To resolve this dilemma, the Food and Emergency Research Unit (FERU) of London, in collaboration with the International

Disasters Institute in London, the Department of Nutrition at the London School of Hygiene and Tropical Medicine and, more recently, with funding from the Independent Commission on International Humanitarian Issues, has conducted promising investigations aimed at developing a low-cost, accurate early-warning system based on field studies carried out first in Ethiopia and subsequently in the Sahelian drought zone and southern Africa.

The FERU Model

FERU's investigations, which reflect to a degree the British colonial experience in 19th-century India that led to the "famine code" based on human rather than crop or weather behavior, demonstrate that indigenous people in Ethiopia have developed survival patterns over decades of hard experience. These patterns enable them to survive long periods of drought—sometimes as long as 8 or 10 years. The research reveals that a series of survival thresholds has to be exhausted before the members of a family, a village or a community leave home and are classified as "famine victims" or "environmental refugees." The survival mechanisms include living off the surpluses of previous "good" years during the first year and, in the second, selling the labor of the older men and boys, while the women walk longer distances to sell what food or household surpluses they feel they can still spare. Early in the process, livestock is sold as grass deteriorates, with draft animals being kept as the last reserve. Eventually, household goods, personal possessions, including jewelry, agricultural equip-ment—excluding the basic tool, the hand hoe—and, finally, weapons will be marketed. If during this process a relief opera-tion is mounted, the men will walk to the distribution center to collect food supplies and return home to eke out the family's precarious existence.

It is only when these mechanisms are exhausted that the members of the community vacate their houses and start walking to the nearest better-off area in search of food and wages. Once the newcomers settle, the inevitable occurs: the market reacts. The volume of cattle being sold increases; therefore livestock prices fall. Food prices increase as demand exceeds supply. In the now-saturated labor market, supply exceeds demand and labor values fall. Unless food is artificially introduced or the rains return, it is only a matter of time before food shortages in the enlarged community, which itself is also enduring drought conditions, become so acute as a result of these pressures that the community falls prey to hunger and is forced, in turn, to move. Thus, small pockets of hunger, each with an acute epicenter but with less stress at the periphery, merge and grow until eventually the government, or the media, declares there is a famine across an entire region. Famine tends to be transmitted in much the same way as an infectious disease might be transmitted. As people walk from one community to the next, the food shortage accompanies them.

If this model holds true, it should be possible to monitor marginal price movements of food and foodstuffs, the volume of cattle sold and the selling of other domestic or household goods in an area under drought stress and to use the data to predict conditions leading to famine.

With the assistance of field staff from private voluntary organizations, FERU is currently testing its thesis. Staff from Save the Children, Oxfam and other organizations are extending the earlier research done in Ethiopia to Sahelian countries and to other parts of sub-Saharan Africa. The early results are encouraging and point to the availability of an inexpensive, accurate system for famine prediction, or early warning. Once the field data is collected, it can be analyzed in a central computer facility and circulated to government and relief agencies.

Averting Disaster

One of the positive characteristics of this imaginative and sensitive model is that it has been established that if the trend leading to famine and migration is spotted early enough, disaster may be averted. To be successful, intervention is required not only in terms of food but more importantly seeds, hoes and modest agricultural equipment, including water pumps and well-drilling equipment. When such remedial action is taken, it can have quite

Famine Forecasting in Northern Ethiopia

Total livestock sales in Korem and Kombolcha markets, Wollo province; Sept. 1981–Jan. 1983.

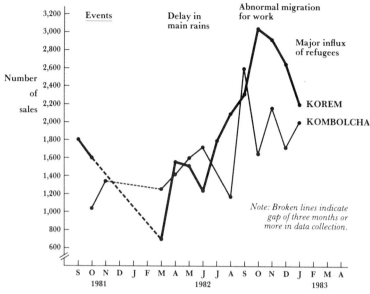

Source: Peter Cutler, "Disasters," Jan. 8, 1984.

dramatic results in delaying and possibly averting famine. The cost of such assistance is minuscule compared with the complex relief operation that has to be mounted once a full-scale famine emergency is declared, as in Ethiopia today. It does, however, require political courage on the part of both the recipient and the donor governments to act decisively in advance of a famine.

Meanwhile human communities are going to have to adapt to the climate of sub-Saharan Africa. The climate cannot be changed or modified, even with significant tree planting. However, human skills and knowledge, including science and inherited or traditional wisdom, can be used to conserve, protect and exploit microclimates at the village or community level. This entails protecting the soil, improving its fertility through organic

23

mulching, reducing albedo (the ratio of reflective energy to solar energy), and helping the farmer to respond with optimum efficiency to what rain does fall and ensuring that water is directed to the roots of plants and trees. Policies can be adopted to ensure that trees, shrubs and grasses are not abused and that human or animal populations are not increased so as to destroy the range ecology. Striking these balances between people and their natural environment is at the heart of successful development in sub-Saharan Africa.

3

'My Son Is My Father'

The human animal is at once ingenious and profligate. He or she has the capacity to exploit the biological carrying systems of nature with such extravagant abandon as to pose a fundamental threat to the natural resource base of the globe itself. The explosive impact of the escalating size of human populations, whose dynamic is measured in terms of a half century and beyond, is in inherent conflict with governments, which typically plan in terms of five-year cycles. This conflict can amount to a formula for immense human suffering. "Whereas it had taken mankind more than a million years to reach a population of one billion, the second billion required only 120 years; the third billion, 32 years; and the fourth billion, 15 years," wrote Robert S. McNamara, former head of the World Bank, in the Summer 1984 issue of *Foreign Affairs*. By the end of the century, a world population of more than 6 billion people will demand a 50 to 60 percent improvement in food output over that of 1980. Nowhere today is this global threat more poignantly obvious than in Africa.

Africa's population is expected to grow from a 1980 figure of 470 million to 853 million by the year 2000. If changes are not immediately implemented, this figure will jump again, to 1.5 billion by 2025, that is, within four decades. UN and World Bank projections anticipate that Africa, which now has some 10 percent of the world's population, will have about 25 percent before global population changes on this scale are complete. While developing countries are growing at an average annual rate of 2.02 percent, Africa is exploding at 3.01 percent per year, according to a 1982 UN assessment.

Policymakers are well aware that population growth figures have little meaning unless related to land availability and land usage. In these terms, the grossly overpopulated countries of the world are Britain, the Netherlands and Japan. But no one in those countries needs to starve to death: land that is privately held is intensively productive, water is abundantly available, organic or chemical inputs are available at prices farmers can afford, storage facilities are plentiful and there are effective mechanisms for market distribution. This is not the case in Africa.

Kenya has the world's highest fertility rate. Between 1980 and 2025, at a 1975 fertility rate of eight per thousand, its population will increase six times to 82.3 million, according to a 1984 FAO report. Half its population today is under the age of 15 years. Kenya is no exception: Rwanda's population will increase five times and Nigeria and Uganda's, four and a half times, each in the same period. Except for localized areas of high sterility, total average fertility rates in Tropical Africa, the region that extends from the Sahara to the Limpopo river, the boundary of southern Africa, are around seven—as high as the world has ever known.

With its current policies, not only can Africa not feed itself, but it is doing profound damage to its biological systems.

Good News and Bad News

Africa has plenty of land—2.9 billion hectares (7.1 billion acres), including South Africa. However, 47 percent of the area is too dry for rain-fed agriculture, and only 19 percent of the soil is free of any inherent limitations on productivity, according to the

FAO. On the other hand, Africa has an enormous potential for rain-fed cropland—some 789 million hectares, excluding marginal land. In 1975 only 168 million hectares of this land, most of which is in the humid tropics, were cultivated. The FAO report states that if these lands had been exploited for food production on a sustainable basis in 1975, the region as a whole, with low inputs of water, fertilizers, improved seeds and the like, would have been capable of supporting 1.12 billion people—three times the actual population. With intermediate inputs, this figure increases to almost 12 times, and, with high inputs, to 34 times. Tragically, a mere 5 percent of development aid currently goes to sustaining and improving this substantial potential for food production.

These continental figures are deceptively encouraging because the potentially productive land is unevenly distributed and includes the rain forests in the Congo Basin, which must not be destroyed. When the figures are broken down on a country-by-country basis, they highlight the problems blocking progress. The World Bank reports that 14 sub-Saharan countries have inadequate amounts of land "to support on a sustainable basis populations as large as those already reached in 1975." Meanwhile, the engine of population growth is roaring ahead, generating a countervailing dynamic.

For countries with individual landholdings, increased family size leads inevitably to the division of holdings and to an increase in smaller plots. The demand made on such plots is too great, good husbandry declines, soil fertility decreases and people are forced onto more-marginal land. The long-term effect of the "Catch 22" situation is disastrous. Demand for fuel wood, especially for the burgeoning cities, escalates. As tree and shrub cover is removed, soil erosion increases and water is no longer held by the foliage or the roots. The water drains off the land, taking the soil with it, into the dams, lakes, rivers and the sea.

Rising Numbers of 'Absolute Poor'

If current policies continue to be pursued, no fewer than 29 of the 64 countries that FAO predicts will be unable to feed their populations by the year 2000 will be African. In 1984–85, 35

African countries received massive food aid. Small wonder, therefore, that urgent attention is paid to slowing down population growth. McNamara states the dilemma succinctly: "Rapid population growth, in sum, translates into rising numbers of labor force entrants, faster-expanding urban populations, pressure on food supplies, ecological degradation, and increasing numbers of 'absolute poor.'" All are rightly viewed by governments as threats to social stability and orderly change. Even under conditions of vigorous economic growth, managing this demographic expansion is difficult; with a faltering economy it is all but impossible. In sub-Saharan Africa, the absolute poor of the region are expected to increase by some 67 percent between now and the year 2000, assuming that meanwhile they do not die. A more rapid fertility decline could hold that increase to some 20 percent.

The argument runs that if India and even China can move significantly in the direction of slowing population growth, Africa can do the same. Immense investments are therefore being made by intergovernmental and private voluntary agencies in family-planning clinics, birth-control programs and the introduction or distribution of various contraceptive devices, from the birth-control pill to abortion, in an attempt to slow down the rate of population expansion.

Deterrents to Slowing Population Growth

Despite some impressive results, notably Zimbabwe's national family-planning program, which has succeeded in raising the use of modern contraceptive methods to 27 percent of fertile women, most policymakers are puzzled that successes, so far, are few and far between. There is a mosaic of reasons. Ignorance plays a significant part. A 1981 Kenya fertility survey revealed that over 55 percent of women interviewed thought that contraceptives would make them ill; 71.4 percent had been under the apprehension that contraception was free when in fact there was a charge for the pills; and 87 percent estimated that getting to a clinic, waiting for attention and returning home would take about six hours. These are all strong deterrents. Kenya is one of the most

Mark Edwards/Earthscan

Wollo Region, Ethiopia: When trees go, wind erosion can make good land worthless.

advanced and politically stable of African countries. Not only is population growth not slowing down, it is increasing. Gill Shepherd, an Oxfam field anthropologist, reports that in the short term "increased field education in Kenya seems to have led to increased fertility, since it leads to the abandonment of traditional contraceptive practices, such as prolonged breast-feeding. Those with primary education have a fertility rate 4 percent higher than those with no schooling."

The most powerful inhibitor to slowing population growth—one that is least understood by policymakers—is the cultural or anthropological factor, including the African's view of God, religion, ancestor worship, lineage, the purpose of the family, witchcraft, marriage, polygamy (which is practiced more in tropical Africa than anywhere else in the world), and the like. Every fertility survey of sub-Saharan Africa demonstrates that when questioned on what size family people would prefer, the usual answer is, "That's up to God." As Africans tell interviewers, "God gives us our children and God takes them away. He decides how many we should have, how many should die and how many should be reborn." Women in Tanzania who had lost their first child—a not uncommon experience—told one reporter in the late 1970s, shortly after the national census, that they had not included that birth/death in their census return because "God gave us our first child and so God has the right to take him [her] away." They felt that the child did not belong to the parents, and certainly not to the state for census purposes. Whether monogamous or polygamous, the root drive remains the same. Fertility is the focus of divine wrath or approval. The Nigerian Edos even address God as "the bringer of children." In many tribes bridal dowry is paid as a spur to reproduction.

There is literally no greater shame for an African woman than to be childless—a clear proof of God's anger. In some tribes, not only will a barren woman be returned to her village of origin in order to avoid "polluting" other women in the village into which she had married, but she will be allocated, on arrival, a hut separated from the main living area. Even her sisters may now be suspect and unacceptable for marriage, so important is the fact of her infertility. Similarly, if a man is known to be sterile, he might be regarded as a sorcerer to be feared, avoided and shunned. At death, barren women and sterile men are often not buried; they may be left in the bush for wild animals to eat.

The 'Ancestral Shades'

In their excellent analysis, "Cultural Forces Tending to Sustain High Fertility in Tropical Africa," John C. Caldwell and Pat Caldwell of the Australian National University write, "The major influence on behavior is not, however, the gods, but the living dead, or ancestral shades, which survive for four or five generations, especially if the proper rites have been performed, and then disappear. . . .These concepts are reinforced by a belief in reincarnation, whereby the dead were born again to their descendants. . . .Children are still given the names of grandparents or great grandparents, and a man will often address his son as his father." If a child dies, the next child is often given his name, and is regarded as "reborn." "Thus to the African, <u>lineage</u> is the fundamental aspect of both society and religion. Each reinforces the other [emphasis added]." A Christian Yoruba taxi driver in Lagos, Nigeria, in 1979 proudly told the author that his father, at 107 years of age, was still alive, although now failing. He then added that although he had married recently, he did not intend to have a child until his father died because "I want a home for his spirit in my first son."

Northern concepts of the ideal family size simply do not exist in Africa; such a concept is alien to that culture. In many regions, women with 12 or more children continue to want more. Large families of 15 to 20 children, except in some pastoral and northern Muslim societies, are not the result of a preference for male children or of planning security for old age. While boys are sometimes preferred to girls for reasons of inheritance, in Ghana the reverse is the case because inheritance passes down the female line. In many regions, the preference is for a balance between the two sexes.

Traditional Birth Control

Traditional mechanisms ensure significant spacing between children. The methods, which protect infant health and help avoid conflict between the duties of mothers and grandmothers within the family, include abstinence from sexual intercourse, long periods of breast-feeding, coitus interruptus (Islamic *azl*), the use of traditional medicines to prevent pregnancy, delayed marriages and women returning to their parents after giving birth and remaining until the child is weaned. Men cannot be accused of adultery in many communities, for theirs is the responsibility of having children in order to secure their lineage. Men often associate contraception with infertility and are more hostile to the idea of birth control than their wives. For women, even the sex act is perceived differently from the way it is perceived in the North. It is neither exciting nor enjoyable, nor is it to be exploited. It simply happens to be the means for having children.

Not surprisingly, therefore, the nuclear family hardly exists. Although the advent of settled farming and schools is steadily eroding the traditional strength of the extended family, children may be fed and may sleep within many houses in the village, where aunts, grandmothers or cousins reside. Long-term planning for children's needs in adulthood is not a powerful motivator.

Since much land in Africa is held in common, often the only way to gain access to land is through children. Land links people to the past as well as to the future, through their children. In much of Tropical Africa the woman is the farmer, and a woman and her children are the basic economic unit. They "sell" their production to the man. In those tribes that live communally in compounds, children ensure access to space within a compound. As women are responsible for child care and child rearing, decisions relating to health, education and early employment are in their hands and reflect their dominant belief system. It is this complex web of interlocking drives that ensures large families in Africa, and essentially it is these drives that family-planning programs must address.

African leaders, despite the fact that some have had distinguished academic careers in developed-world universities, continue to be deeply rooted inevitably—and some would argue correctly—in the mores of traditional African beliefs. No African leader has effectively addressed the issues of family planning, even in those areas where the teaching of family planning has taken root and created a demand for contraceptive devices and family-planning support services.

Recommended: A Long-term Strategy

The cultural factors at play in the field of family planning represent the tip of a very complex and powerful iceberg. The interplay between family, land, religion, politics, power, prestige and status are far-reaching, daunting and fundamentally African. Against this formidable and deep-seated subculture, the random distribution of pills and condoms is irrelevant as well as insulting. But there are two countervailing forces that may ultimately have the effect of persuading Africans to have smaller families. One is imported religions, namely Christianity and Islam, which offer

Colin Jones/Earthscan

In Tropical Africa women raise families, farm, harvest and process food. Grinding flour alone takes many hours.

different sets of values. Second, the economic process itself, provided it improves, will erode traditional beliefs. In both cases, 25 to 50 years may elapse before significant changes manifest themselves, and, as in the North, improved economic prosperity that ultimately leads to smaller families first generates an increase in numbers before family size "peaks." In the meantime:

▶ Social and cultural anthropologists versed in African value systems should play a dominant role in any Northern-funded family-planning program for Africa.

▶ Men should be a prime target of such educational programs, with family-planning advice but one weapon in the armory. The approach should focus on self-help groups of farmers or villagers, with the blessing and presence of the elders or chiefs. Family-planning programs standing on their own, not integrated into a range of development activities, should be abolished as ineffective and insensitive. The needs of adulthood in terms of land usage should be a dominant theme.

▶ Where such culturally sensitive programs have taken root—and these are not inconsiderable, particularly among women—there needs to be a more consistent supply of cheap contraceptives, easily obtainable, preferably from women with whom they are familiar and who taught them family-planning techniques.

▶ Because of the strength of polygamy and traditional beliefs, single working girls in the growing cities could be a focus of special, ongoing campaigns in favor of the use of the pill and similar contraceptive devices.

▶ New studies should be conducted to devise ways, means and arguments for building on, and using, the given traditional beliefs in respect to children—that they are a "gift from God" and hence should not be abused.

▶ The relative openness of the African to imported culture represents an opportunity for the advancement of new ideas. It follows that children in schools, colleges and universities represent a special opportunity. Key opinion-formers, particularly political leaders (local as well as national), field educators, church leaders, doctors and nurses, need to be convinced of the efficacy of family planning and to exploit their role in promoting it.

▶ U.S. funding for culturally sensitive, family-planning programs in Africa should be restored, and a special, sustained effort should be made to supply families with contraceptive and other family-planning services where earlier educational programs have created a demand. U.S. policy should not pivot on a single issue like abortion, which, in any case, is traditionally abhorred in Africa. Recent U.S. policies barring aid to organizations that "support coercive abortion programs or participate in their management" have discouraged family-planning advocates, but they have had little effect, except to isolate the United States itself. Ultimately Africans, not Americans or Europeans, must decide upon policy in this sensitive and personal area of human experience.

Virtually all these recommendations relate to a longer-term strategy. It is probable that increasing food production in Africa has a higher potential for promoting a higher quality of life in the short-to-intermediate term than reducing population figures.

4

First, Food to Eat

If one of the first tests of good government is the capacity either to grow or to purchase enough food to satisfy the basic nutritional and dietary needs of the people, then, with the possible exception of countries like Botswana, Cameroon, the Ivory Coast, Malawi, Rwanda and Burundi, the record of sub-Saharan Africa since the late 1960s is one of dismal failure.

Although Africa was largely self-sufficient in food production in the 1960s, during the 1970s overall production of major food crops fell by 14 percent, according to FAO estimates. Today food production is growing at only 1.8 percent per year, compared to an annual population increase of 3.01 percent, according to a 1984 World Bank report. Twenty percent of cereal requirements has to be imported. Between 1970 and 1980, the cost of those imports increased a staggering 600 percent.

Food aid to Africa increased on average by 9.5 percent annually in the 1970s. In human terms, this meant that one out of every five Africans became dependent for survival on food aid and their tastes changed as a result. There has been a huge increase in demand for wheat and maize (234 percent from 1965–67 and 207 percent from 1975–77 to 1985) in the Sahel, where local wheat production meets only 2 percent of requirements.

There is no dignity or real salvation in food aid. Neither food imports nor food aid on this scale solves the problem. At least 20 percent of Africans continue to be malnourished: they are forced to tolerate calorie levels that are below the minimum essential to good health. According to UNICEF, some 5 million children died in 1984 from hunger-related diseases. That figure was expected to double in 1985.

Food aid is also very difficult to handle. In the drought-stricken area of Darfur in Sudan, impoverished farmers, having no seeds to plant, decided when rain fell in 1985 to use seed taken from food-aid sorghum supplied by the United States. Some of it germinated and will produce a harvest of sorts. But U.S. sorghum is mostly a first-generation hybrid—so is genetically regressive. Their harvest will be poor. If they repeat the process of sowing some seed from what is harvested, the next harvest will be virtually nonexistent.

It is easy to identify the key factors in this bleak synopsis. Population growth is one. Political instability is another. Since 1945, Black Africa has endured 73 political coups and has witnessed the assassination of 13 heads of state. Africa in 1984 for the first time imported more arms than food. During the past three years, while U.S. food aid to Africa increased by 40 percent, U.S. military aid to the hungriest continent in the world jumped by 150 percent, with 36 African nations receiving military aid, compared with only 19 in 1981, wrote Jack Shepherd in the April 1984 issue of *The Atlantic*. During the past two years, bread riots have taken place in countries as far apart as Morocco, Tunisia, Sudan, Ghana and Uganda.

As civil unrest accompanies a decline in soil fertility, reinforced by the growth of arid and desert zones, it is little wonder that 1 in every 250 Africans is a refugee. Having only a tenth of the world's population, Africa is generating a quarter of the dispossessed of the world, according to the World Bank.

People from the Karal Region of Chad travel with all their belongings in search of water.

Flawed Development Policies

While these factors, plus the debt crisis, commodity-price decline and the colonial legacy are important, a major contributory responsibility for the misery of Africans lies with the development policies adopted by the larger multilateral and bilateral agencies and supported eagerly by African governments.

Goesta Edgren, under-secretary of state of the Swedish Foreign Ministry, when speaking at the International Institute for Environment and Development Conference in London in 1985 on the African crisis confessed, "As a result of an inappropriate choice of technology, the Swedish rural water programs in Tanzania and Kenya have reached what must be termed a dead end. After 15 years of quite considerable investment in piped water and mechanized pumping equipment, hardly more than 10 percent of our installations are still in use." Not only has much large-scale aid been inappropriate, it frequently has also been politically oriented, without regard for people's needs. Often it has been ineffective in helping people to stand on their own feet, using their own community and environmental resources to secure their salvation, and has been destructive of community life. Despite the rigors of desertification, only 1.4 percent of aid to the Sahel has gone into reforestation schemes. Only 4 percent of development aid has gone to rain-fed agriculture. And yet improving farming techniques in terms of environment, seed strain, marketing and storage ought to be the top priority of virtually every African government.

Over 70 percent of Africans live in rural areas as subsistence farmers. Most live on small farms of 2 to 10 acres. Land is communally held within the tribe or, in a minority of cases, privately owned. Traditionally, land clearance followed by up to eight years of fallow, when reinforced with intercropping, has enabled farmers to retain their soil, to hold its moisture content and to control or even eliminate its weeds. There is little systematic irrigation and not much use of high-energy inputs, like fertilizers or pesticides. Cattle and other livestock, which can be critical to the local economy, especially in the arid or semiarid zones, are used for plowing in mixed farming areas. They also provide a source of protein to the family and cash when sold on the market. If water is made available through wells, bunds or dams, livestock can multiply, encouraged by herdsmen who regard them as their prime source of wealth, to the point that they destroy the range ecology. This occurred in the Karamoja region of Uganda immediately following independence. While traditional technologies result in lower yields per hectare compared with averages in other parts of the world, they have been broadly adequate in the past in meeting people's needs.

The appropriate development model is likely to be one that builds upon this solid base, taps into the traditional wisdom, moves at a pace acceptable to the rural poor, recognizes the central role played by women, offers cash benefits and credits to the rural poor, uses high-energy processes most sparingly, if at all, and is sensitive to African culture. In short, development should be small-scale, low-intensity and seek a balance between

Ethiopians prepare the soil to plant seedlings at a tree nursery in
the Doba catchment area east of Addis Ababa in a
government-sponsored effort to restore depleted vegetation.

human ecology and the range ecology. Unhappily, this is the
antithesis of much of the assistance provided by Northern governments. Under the impetus first of the colonial administrations and
then, in postindependence years, of major multilateral donors
with the exception of the World Bank, Black Africa increasingly
has become geared to cash-crop exports. (Seventy-five percent of
World Bank aid has been for food production.)

Since 1970, the Sahelian drought zone has been generating
more agricultural produce than ever before, but in the form of
commodities rather than food to eat. In Upper Volta in the 1960s,
cotton output totaled only 2,000 tons per year; in 1984, it reached
75,000 tons. Mali has a comparable record in cotton and peanuts
for export, and Chad, in cotton. Ghana in 1980 actively discouraged farmers from producing more food when it pegged the price

of rice at roughly 50 percent its local market value, thereby destroying the small rural farmers' incentive. The government further discouraged farmers from increasing their output when it accepted food aid. Ethiopia similarly has set some food prices at less than the cost to produce it. When allied to a system that requires a person to farm land that may belong to someone else the next year, Ethiopia's policy is demoralizing. By contrast, when Uganda doubled food prices by presidential decree in 1983, it resulted in a 400 percent increase in locally produced food.

Prescription for Development

Africa has now deteriorated to such an extent that it presents an acute humanitarian challenge to the rest of the world. If tens of millions of Africans are not to starve to death between now and the end of the century, a small, central core of simple yet profound changes must be pursued relentlessly and vigorously.

▶ There must be a recognition that there are no short-term solutions to Africa's dilemma. The typical two-to-five-year project favored by private voluntary organizations and governments alike is wholly inadequate to the continent's needs. Strategies and programs must replace projects. Programs should be conceived in terms of a 50-year strategy and planned within a period of a decade or longer. Degraded land alone takes at least 25 years to recover, and population changes take even longer to work themselves through. Where political exigencies allow, programs must relate to natural regional groupings and not to the artificial and largely meaningless sovereign boundaries generated by the unfortunate Conference of Berlin. The Horn of Africa is a natural unit. So are the Sahel, southern Africa, the moist rain-forest areas of Central Africa, the revived East African community or the more-temperate Mediterranean coastal lands of the north.

In this context, the thrust of the Lagos plan of action for the economic development of Africa, adopted by the Organization of African Unity in 1980, is more likely to result in success than the steps outlined in the World Bank's 1981 report, *Accelerated Development in Sub-Saharan Africa: An Agenda for Action,* by Dr. Elliot Berg and others. The Berg plan, with its emphasis on domestic policy reform, population planning, increased external assistance supported by pricing and budgeting changes, and the strange assumption that on the whole basic goods and services are in place, when patently they are not, is a Northern view of what Africa should do. It is likely to lead to food-aid dependency and little real change for the rural poor. The World Bank's more recent guidance document, *Towards Sustained Development in Sub-Saharan Africa*, looks for policy reform by donors as well as recipients and is a step in the right direction.

The Lagos plan is authentically African and builds upon African strengths. It has prompted 34 African countries to design national food strategies, and 12 countries are now actually implementing them. Progress is being made, although it remains to be seen how far food strategies conceived nationally can be made to work to help the small farmers and the landless—for that is the real test of success.

▶ The key target now must be to "grow food to eat" by tapping the human energy and creativity within village and community and the traditional wisdom and inherited knowledge. The small-scale farmers of Africa cannot afford to risk their meager resources in technological innovation, monocropping or high-energy agriculture. Human labor, principally that of women and children, is the basic input. Hand hoes should be used instead of plows, and draft cattle, or sometimes camels, instead of tractors. Weed and pest control should be handled by symbiosis or smothering instead of crop spraying; and small village storage facilities, with losses held to 4 or 5 percent, should be used instead of large temperature- and humidity-controlled silos. This mix of the cultural and the ecological, when allied to a mobilization of the rural people, will turn Africa around and move the continent back to prosperity.

It may be argued that the "poorest of the poor" have been the target of many large donor agencies for a decade or more. That is true. But it is also true that such agencies have rarely recruited the staff committed to that concept. They have been unable or unwilling to develop the precision of focus which makes it possible to produce dramatic results by applying very small grants, $10,000 and less. Such precision requires patience, skill and considerable empathy for the community in which the funder is operating. To throw money at problems solves nothing. Grants that act like fertilizer to the seed or like a lubricant to the pump tend to be the ones that are culturally sensitive and mobilize the people themselves.

People will use their own energies and creative powers only if they are fully consulted and participate directly in designing and implementing their own development. Robert Chambers is right when he argues in the February 1985 issue of *Disaster* that "for all the rhetoric about participation, it is still rare enough for villages, let alone the poorer people in villages, to be consulted about their priorities, or if they are consulted, for their preferences to be a source of learning and official action." Ideally, aid should not be "for" the poor; it should be "by" the poor.

Credit facilities, including small revolving loan funds, storage facilities, improved hand tools, a steady supply of reliable seeds, better access to markets and, above all, a fair pricing structure for surplus crops will all help to turn Africa's basic economy around. Credit and better prices, however, will motivate only if basic goods (soap, salt, bicycles, transistor radios, oil and the like) are available in the shops of small villages. Currently, these basic necessities are missing.

▶ Since women provide 60 to 80 percent of the labor (the planting, weeding, harvesting, processing and storing), donor aid programs should support them to the hilt. Women in Africa are forced to spend inordinate periods of time grinding corn and carrying water or wood. In Burkina Faso, women often spend all the hours between dawn and noon collecting water and carrying it back home. In Sudan, grinding maize can be a four-to-five-hour job each day; in Tanzania, collecting firewood can consume the same time, while preparing food on inefficient fires can take two to three hours per day with all the attendant problems of safety for small children. Labor-saving devices in these areas, based on low-cost and simple tools for carrying or processing, would pay large dividends if the time saved was then spent on growing and tending crops.

A woman pounds millet in the Majia Valley of south Niger.

Kitchen vegetable gardens, using proven microcatchment techniques, which provide essential dietary requirements for the cooking pot, need more support and research. As in the rest of the world, such personally owned "allotments" have a yield per acre far higher than "field" or "plantation" crops. Similarly, a string of intensive, localized cropping techniques in urban areas, including composting, aquaculture and small ground or rooftop gardens, can help to supplement diets and make a significant contribution to food sufficiency. Private voluntary organizations like Oxfam, the American Friends Service Committee and the Peace Corps have had successful experiences with women-oriented support programs throughout both rural and urban Africa.

If agricultural extension services could more effectively focus on women, a minor revolution would take place. As UNICEF and Oxfam have demonstrated in Ethiopia, the poor treat cash handouts, if they are equitably distributed, with honor and prudence and put them to wise and effective use. Although women usually have little to offer in the form of collateral to credit agencies, the standard of honesty of the very poor is exceptionally high, with a 90 or 95 percent rate of repayment. Credit stimulates the local economy and brings about a qualitative change in village life. Political courage is needed to engage in such a process. Women themselves should be trained and equipped to act as extension service agents, because many African men refuse to talk to women farmers or to give them their support. The effectiveness of this approach has been proved in the Sahel and in the Horn of Africa. It is the larger donors who need to study these examples and replicate them.

Appropriate Agricultural Research

Many donor agencies have poured funds into agricultural research institutions in Africa over a number of decades. The gains are modest in the extreme. Kenya alone has at least 25 such research centers. Yet environmental degradation in northern Kenya and, as a consequence, human suffering are every bit as severe there as in the Horn of Africa or the Sahel. Clearly, the greater part of the research undertaken is either inefficient or inappropriate. The aim has been to bend the environment to suit the needs of the plant (if the soil is too dry, water it; if it lacks nutrients, fertilize it), whereas what is needed is to find plants that can be made to fit the fragile and vulnerable environment of Africa. Dr. Norman Myers, African field specialist, is right to argue that what is required is not a Green Revolution but a "gene" revolution.

Although the International Crops Research Institute for the Semi-Arid Tropics established its main African program only in 1982, it has produced a type of millet that was the only one to survive the 1984 drought in Sudan. AID has funded new and successful research into improving both cassava and sorghum—essential to Africa's food sufficiency. Despite these successes and those achieved through the Consultative Group for International Agricultural Research (CGIAR), Africa still needs to improve these and other traditional foodstuffs—sweet potatoes, yams and white maize. It can learn from Asia, which researched and improved rice strains appropriate to the eating habits of Asians. Intercropping with nitrogen-fixing plants, a cheap supply of drought-resistant seed and techniques of pest/disease control through the use of the symbiotic relationship of certain plants or plants and insects should all be central to African research. Although CGIAR allocates some 37 percent of its budget to sub-Saharan Africa, little is spent on these crucial, self-help techniques. In one recent year, research into the staple food of maize attracted a derisory $23 million. Coffee, conversely, attracted $39 million. In 1983, the British aid program allocated £15,000 to research on millet, but twice as much to tobacco improvement in Malawi alone.

One would assume that in a drought-stricken continent, techniques of irrigation would be well-researched and taught to village communities. This is not the case. Virtually no work has been done on this critical subject except by private voluntary organizations. The target for small-scale farmers, as for the landless, is to secure stability of performance in food production—to avoid risk, rather than to maximize output. In one area of Tanzania, small farmers traditionally grow 24 different kinds of rice, thus spreading the risk. Research should support and exploit these priorities.

There has been little or no research on soil even though at least a decade of basic research is likely to be necessary to improve the continent's low soil fertility and to tackle parasites like Striga, which attaches itself to the roots of millet and sorghum, greatly reducing yields.

Soil conservation is another critical area that is grossly under-researched, along with techniques like minimum tillage or no tillage. Kenya is pioneering an interesting soil conservation program using mulching and contour-farming techniques. The program, wisely, is likely to be spread over two decades. Belatedly, Ethiopia is developing a series of effective terracing programs to conserve the fast-disappearing soil in its highland territory. Every country or region should be following suit.

African students and scientists, versed in their own cultural sensitivities, should above all begin to replace expatriate scientists as rapidly as possible. Crash teaching programs, with follow-up research in African rather than Northern universities or field stations, should be built into donor programs. The "barefoot doctor" approach should be fostered assiduously within agricultural extension services, and local regions should help write the actual agendas of research stations set up in their midst.

Donor agencies should insist that extension officers spend the bulk of their time in the villages and fields in order to get away from the all-too-typical situation that finds them trapped in the capital city having no vehicle, maintenance parts or petrol. Too often, when petrol and vehicle spares are available, elitist extension workers continue to stick to the "tarmacadam," never venturing into the heartland. Yet it is there and there alone that changes in favor of first growing food to eat before it is grown for profit will be made. That is the essential step in turning Africa around. Examples of what can be done already exist. It is by no means an impossible task.

5

Human Capital Investment

While Africa's problems can best be resolved by Africans themselves, the North and the large donor agencies have a crucial support role to play and a contribution to make. Slashing the budgets of the International Development Association, the International Fund for Agricultural Development, or even the United Nations Educational, Scientific and Cultural Organization (UNESCO) merely inhibits sustainable development, exacerbates the problems and ensures that genuine progress will be retarded. Eventually, because we live in one world and are interdependent, the consequences of reducing aid will adversely affect the North as well as the South.

The statistical data constructed by experts to describe the root of Africa's spiraling rate of developmental and environmental bankruptcy have little intellectual underpinning. The figures produced must nevertheless be used to illustrate the argument, as has been done in the preceding chapters. No African government, and certainly no development agency, knows, within any acceptable margin of error, either the birthrate, the mortality rate or the food production of any African state. Yet these three figures are critical to the success or failure of any sustainable development program. In the North, statisticians are willing to accept up to a 10 percent variable in assessing food-production needs and actual production. In Africa, an error of 30 percent or higher is not uncommon. Such variables make nonsense of rational budgetary or planning exercises.

In his seminal book, *Nature Pleads Not Guilty*, Rolando Garcia estimates that during the last Ethiopian famine, merchants in the capital city of Addis Ababa sold between 750,000 and 800,000 tons of grain they had stored, while Northern relief agencies shipped in 1.2 million tons of grain. People were dying of starvation, but was there a famine? Or is it necessary to redefine what is meant by a famine? In July 1985, food could be bought in Tigre and Wollo in Ethiopia, and food trading was going on in Sudan where there was widespread hunger.

Diagnosis and Cure

If development is to be sustainable, diagnoses, despite statistical inadequacies, must precede effective treatment. And any program that is not sustainable is at best worth pursuing only in terms of short-term, humanitarian relief—what the medieval scholars called "binding up the wounds of suffering humanity."

In terms of basic needs, ideology has helped little in Africa. During the past 30 years, Marxist, capitalist, socialist and mixed economic models in Africa have suffered broadly the same defects, have experienced the same failures and have misfired in moving the people forward in much the same way. The poor of Tanzania, Kenya, Angola or South Africa therefore face approximately the same bleak, uncompromising future. The African poverty trap treats competing doctrinaire ideologies with much the same contempt.

There comes a time in the crisis-ridden history of any nation when survival depends upon one crucial factor: inspiring and motivating the people to repel the enemy and to improve their condition. The Victorian social reformer John Ruskin noted that "the wealth of a country is in its good men and women and in nothing else." And he was right. Ultimately, the only secure,

Villagers walk across a dry riverbed in Banjagara, Mali.

renewable asset Africa has is its people. People and their governments cause famines, not the climate or the environment. People and their governments can prevent or resolve famines if they so choose. That is why the policies of emphasizing basic needs at the village level, as adopted in the last two or three years by the leaders of Niger (General Seyni Kountche), Burkina Faso (Captain Thomas Sankara) and possibly Ghana (Captain Jerry Rawlings) are encouraging. These men are attempting to demonstrate what can be done if leaders build from the bottom up, using the strengths of their rural populations, operating by example and tackling vigorously governmental corruption and bureaucratic inertia.

Capital investment in human resources offers the alternative way forward in Africa. Such investment will take many forms and shapes—a mosaic of initiatives referred to in the preceding chapters rather than the linear development promoted by economists and treasury officials. In jargonistic terms, what is required is the holistic, interdisciplinary process of human development that strikes a balance between people, their communities and their environment.

The capacity to survive, and to survive with an impressive buoyancy of spirit, represents one of the two assets with which Africa can build its own distinctive future. The other asset is the carrying systems of nature. Africa is a continent of sunshine, water, soil, forests, vegetation and natural animal stock in great abundance. That the balance is hideously wrong today does not deny the basic proposition. It follows that to reclaim arid zones and to halt the spread of the desert by helping people and their communities represents the best strategy if Africa is to escape from the poverty trap.

Four Points to Ponder

From this perspective, four key points are worth pondering. First, poverty is the principal enemy of the people, not drought or famine. People are poor in a market economy because they have no surplus cash in their pockets to spend and, in Africa, no goods or services on which to spend it if they had it. They are poor because the economic system within which they must live frustrates their efforts to escape from the poverty trap. They are poor because the rich and the powerful do not listen to them and in fact count them of little importance.

Malnutrition, disease, illiteracy, squalor—that is "poverty"—ensure that the human potential in either its individual or collective manifestation is never realized. Poverty creates vulnerability, and vulnerability translates in social terms into powerlessness. Basic needs have to be met before Africans can cease to be vulnerable and begin to realize their potential. This is the second point.

Third, agriculture must return to basics. The pattern of traditional agriculture of Kenya's Kikuyu was based upon intercropping beans, potatoes and maize. Thirty years ago, development agencies persuaded the Kikuyu to practice single cropping, with lower-quality results. Today, the Kikuyu are reverting to the traditional pattern, with increased yields, better pest control and effective weed control. The geneticist, the plant breeder and the proponent of the Green Revolution have an important contribution to make. But one of the most precious threads woven into the cultures of traditional Africa is inherited knowledge, particularly in the fields of agriculture and medicine. This knowledge has immediate and potential relevance to the future. There is mumbo jumbo, witchcraft and trickery within those cultural knowledge banks, but there are also pearls of wisdom.

Among traditional pastoralists in the Sahel, various researchers have shown that levels of livestock production of protein per hectare compare more than favorably with capital-intensive systems in the United States and Australia. Technology can teach these herders little. For centuries, the Masai and other tribal herdsmen based decisions related to rainfall on the behavior of the Siafru, or Safari ant. Within three weeks of rains, the Safari ant moves to the winged phase of its reproductive cycle. Traditional farmers likewise knew that the flowering of the acacia tree, the Breuistica Spika, would occur one month before the rains. When arid zones were spotted with trees covered with white blossoms, it was time to move cattle. Across the continent as a whole, the average African can select his or her diet from a range of a hundred vegetables and fruits. An American is limited to a far smaller range. More important, the traditional diet of the African is healthier than that of the Northerner, with a noticeable absence on the continent of illnesses like bowel cancer and heart attack.

Traditional medicine offers a host of similar insights. In western Africa, cassava is fermented to get rid of its toxic cyanide content; in Ethiopia, cereals are put through a similar fermenting process that heightens and improves protein content. Dr. John Rivers of the London School of Hygiene and Tropical Medicine, intrigued by the use of spices and curries in food preparation in Ethiopia and yet puzzled by how and why poor people continued to spend money on spices, brought samples home for analysis and further investigation. He discovered that the spices act as powerful and effective antibacterial agents. Thus meat treated in this manner could be kept safely for long periods of time. Rivers reports that so potent was this insight that major food processors in Britain are showing commercial interest in the technique for their own products. In the West African rain forest there grows a plant called *katemje,* which local Africans have been using for centuries to sweeten tea, wine and sour breads. In fact, katemje seeds produce the world's sweetest known compound. Molecule for molecule, it is 100,000 times sweeter than sugar and, on a weight basis, 3,000 times sweeter.

The fourth point is that the entire international and national aid program ought now to be swung in the direction of Africa's rural poor. The second half of the equation, pursuing policies to balance the needs of the people with the strength of nature's carrying systems, is equally crucial to Africa's future. If water tables are depleted, neither crops nor people can thrive. The lesson is simple: when people get too far out of step with nature, they are likely to face a difficult future.

The dynamic for change that Africa's environmental crisis has triggered should be recognized and used. The Chinese character for "crisis" recognizes that "opportunity" is always present in "crisis." "There is no more powerful force for progress against poverty than the initiative and ingenuity of poor people themselves," A.W. Clausen, president of the World Bank, recently declared. If governments and major aid agencies shifted their development policies toward the landless and the small-scale rural producer and her community with its priorities, while significantly improving the physical and economic infrastructure in those areas beyond the reach of village communities or private voluntary donors, the desert could be made to bloom, the soil could be given back its fertility, water could be husbanded and used to optimum effect, and labor-intensive agriculture could reemerge. The real challenge therefore is to interpret Northern concepts of "sustainable agriculture" and even "sustainable development" in terms of action within local communities, which gives rise to what Chambers has correctly defined as "sustainable livelihoods." At the end of the day, it is livelihoods which really matter.

On the strength of success achieved in the basic areas of health, education, literacy and finally the wise exploitation of cash crops and mineral resources there could be laid the foundations of a prosperous, modern economy, shaped and molded to the cultural norms of the African people. At last "development" would become "authentic."

The North does not have the right to play with the poor for either economic or security reasons. Absolute poverty has to be abolished because it is morally wrong and because it is a cul-de-sac for both the donors and the recipients of aid. Sustainable development for day-by-day living is the way forward for Africa. Any alternative will merely twist the spiral deeper into poverty and irreversible environmental bankruptcy.

Three Case Histories

Water Harvesting and Agro-forestry in the Yatenga, Burkina Faso

An Oxfam Project Report

Rainwater runs off arid impermeable soil and is lost, taking valuable topsoil with it. In 1979 Oxfam initiated an experiment in Burkina Faso aimed at capturing this run-off rainfall and using it for tree planting. Farmers subsequently adapted the water-harvesting techniques. Fields long abandoned are being reclaimed, and farmers are increasing water infiltration and gradually building up soil depth. Those villages which have adopted some of the project's ideas are now used as demonstration centers and provide training for neighboring villages.

The Project's Origin

Before joining Oxfam's field staff, Bill Hereford had spent several years in the U.S. Peace Corps on a well-digging program in Burkina Faso. He had lived through drought years and good years, seeing crops prosper and fail. He had also observed women trekking further and further to get firewood. Firewood prices in the capital of Ouagadougou had escalated sharply over the years.

Convinced that something had to be done to grow more trees and conserve scarce water, Hereford spent part of a vacation visiting the Negev area of Israel. There he saw trees growing in the desert, each in its own rectangular or saucer-shaped micro-catchment area—an age-old method of using scarce rainfall. He returned to Burkina Faso determined to introduce their technique.

Hereford persuaded Oxfam to design a program and hire technical staff, something Oxfam rarely does. The next step, in early 1979, was to arrange for a soil expert to measure the water filtration and storage capacities of the soil. A Peace Corps forester, Arlene Blade, was hired in July, and by mid-August the team reported "300 microcatchments spread through 8 villages in the Yatenga. Trials under way since May with 20 species—tree/bush and tree/vine associations. Also trying rice in the microcatchment with a tree."

A month later, Hereford wrote, "The most encouraging aspect is that the villages have given unstinting support despite the fact that they are busy with their food crops. Arlene has sensibly arranged for the tree planting to take place in the evening when people are coming home from the fields. (The microcatchments were constructed earlier, in the dry season, when people had more time.) The selected species satisfy one or all of the following criteria: that they produce an edible fruit or nut, that their foliage be edible and nutritious for man and/or animal, and that they be valuable as a soil retention/regeneration agent because of their root system and/or the fertilizer value of their foliage."

Obtaining seeds and plants was not easy. Sometimes plants suffered in transport, and on one occasion they were planted in their plastic bags and promptly died. Of the 24 species that were grown and carefully monitored, 7 failed miserably and fewer than one fourth survived. Eight, including some local species, were selected for future use. They were propagated in a local government tree nursery in Ouahigouya and in a nursery set up by a women's group in one of the villages.

Ask the Women

In the second year of the program, Arlene drew up a questionnaire to find out from the villagers what tree and shrub species were least favored by domestic animals (goats, sheep and cattle) and which species made the best firewood. The answers were fascinating.

Several of the preferred species were among the initial plantings, but many on the firewood list were new. The latter consisted mainly of shrubs: they were preferred because they are easier to reach and cut and regenerate more quickly. Some were selected because they were fast-drying, others because they burned well, with few sparks and little smoke. The women, with the experience of generations, knew their firewood. Nine species were eventually selected for the program; of the nine, five were also on the list of plants that were known to be least favored by domestic animals.

Learning from Experience

The survival rates of the trees and bushes continued to be poor; many were eaten by animals. To protect the plants, various fencing techniques were tried, using both live and dead materials: barbed wire, waste-metal strips and woven branches from trees and bushes. But fencing cost time and money and threatened to undermine the program, as it had so many tree-planting schemes in other parts of the world. That was why it was so important to plant shrubs disliked by animals.

When a new request for funds was put to Oxfam in May 1981, the program had already begun expanding, "with farmers actively involved in designing and remodeling" it, according to field director Brendan Gormely. "The main thrust is now toward using a wide range of soil-conservation techniques aimed at increasing agricultural output, rather than limiting it to a reafforestation program." Contrary to the original soil scientist's advice to grow only trees in the microcatchments for best water use, the farmers were growing food crops with the bushes and modifying the catchment size and shape.

Catchments and Crops

Three main types of catchment emerged: the original ones brought from Israel and suitable for flat land; a crescent-shaped enclosure varying in length from 3 to 10 meters—the simplest and most economical form of construction; and a series of low embankments or ridges 4 to 10 inches high made of stones, earth or even millet stalks or other vegetable matter—the most adaptable. These are constructed on flat land or along the contours on sloping land at intervals of 10 to 30 yards.

The sites chosen have in the main been areas in or on the outskirts of villages that were once cultivated or grew bushes and trees. Now they are hard and barren, with topsoil washed away and sometimes with a covering of small stones.

As the catchments are developed, the farmers have been planting rice, maize, sorghum, millet and groundnuts—different crops in different villages. The international dry lands research organization, ICRISAT, has been brought in to monitor and advise on the crops.

Spreading the Word

"The transfer of ideas from project personnel to farmers was accomplished by word of mouth, demonstrations, observations of others' work and simple collective headscratching. . . . The network of farmers has tended to grow each year to cover about 30 village groups," wrote the project director in July 1982. "And at least 130 individual farmers are practicing some of the project's methods in their personal fields."

The project has also maintained excellent links with the forestry services, which adopted its reforestation techniques so that Oxfam could drop the latter from its program. There has been excellent cooperation with the local government's rural development organization as well, and field staff are investigating possibilities of linking up with another nongovernmental organization that works in some of the villages.

In August 1982 Oxfam approved funds for two more years. The program was extended to a third subdivision of Yatenga, and training centers were established in the "best villages" using the most successful farmers for teaching. Experimentation and testing of new ideas, like direct seeding (instead of tree nurseries), the use of green mulches, spacing between embankments, water retention and so on, continued.

"No operational agency, government or private, was willing to undertake the initial trials, either of the techniques themselves or of the approach that put the farmer as the key person in the equation. So we were forced to go it alone," wrote Brendan Gormley. "We are trying to downgrade the role of the technician. . .using the villages where the techniques are well understood to act as host and trainer for individuals or villages wanting to learn the techniques. In exchange for the teaching, the pupils will work for free on the land of the host village. . . .

"A project that started as a technical one has now blossomed into a social and organizational one, with our role that of liaison and organization. The fact that Oxfam is now the leader in this field means that we have a responsibility to carry on, especially as it is the farmers themselves who are proving that if the mix is right and if they are interested in what is happening, more-sophisticated aid theories and practices become irrelevant."

Oxfam's contribution to the program from 1978 to 1982 came to £41,438 ($59,256 at the current rate of exchange).

Development in Guinea-Bissau

*An American Friends Service Committee
Report Project*

Guinea-Bissau is one of the six poorest nations in the world, and the poorest of the poor are the country's rural women. The American Friends Service Committee's Women and Development Program, which began work in Guinea-Bissau in 1980, seeks to improve the quality of life for rural women and their families by introducing time-saving, labor-saving devices and by promoting activities that will help them earn some income.

Agricultural Project at Geba

Even though women spend most of their time growing, harvesting, processing and preparing food for the family, with proper support they could increase their yields both in quantity and quality. They need equipment to prepare and cultivate the soil (oxen would suffice), better access to water, disease-resistant seeds, technical advice. Even more important, AFSC staff say, they need recognition by the government and by men in general of their importance and their contribution to subsistence farming.

Guinea-Bissau's Department of Agriculture asked AFSC to help implement a two-year experimental horticultural project on land the government had assigned to rural women at Geba. In the past year some 500 women along with staff members of Guinea-Bissau's Department of Agriculture have transformed the land along the Geba river into farmland, enabling women to raise more vegetables for their families and a surplus to sell in the market. AFSC provided garden tools, seeds and technical help, as well as 15 bicycles for government extension workers and a truck to transport vegetables to nearby towns and to the capital, Bissau.

As director Paulette Nichols explained AFSC's objectives: "Quaker Service is not here to show rural women how to grow vegetables, how to care for their children, or how to increase their income. Quaker Service's role is to provide basic tools, materials and training to complement their efforts. Rural women were growing vegetables long before our presence, yet their tools were few, worn or nonexistent. They lacked a variety of seeds or they had a short supply."

The project ran into some unforeseen complications. Onions are a rare commodity in Guinea-Bissau: a large onion sells for $4 to $5. Onions were stolen in the night from the gardens, which are outside the village. Discouraged, many women stopped watering the onions before they reached medium size, pulled them out and stored them, selling a few a day. This year Quaker Service will ask the government for guards, and it is likely to get them because onions produced domestically reduce the need for imports. Once there are plenty of onions on the market, the price will fall, making them less attractive to thieves.

Women Gardeners near Bissau

For several years, approximately 130 women have grown vegetables on the state farm outside Bissau, where there is sufficient water and fertile land. The women have worked small individual plots, sharing buckets (old tin cans) and tools. They supplied 90 percent of the produce sold at the local market, yet they received little or no help from the agricultural department which manages the farm. AFSC provided the women with equipment and seeds, and the quantity, quality and sales of produce grew rapidly. The project was so successful that the local agricultural department initiated a citywide women's gardening project. The rural extension workers who have been helping the women on the state farm were asked to coordinate the new project, which will include the state farm gardeners.

Regional Exchange

Whenever possible, AFSC provides women with an opportunity to meet and learn from each other. Last year four Guinean women from the Ministries of Rural Development, Health and Education took part in a four-week study tour in Mozambique and Zimbabwe. They learned about new approaches and technologies in such areas as vegetable growing and rabbit raising, and they met women with whom they could exchange information in the future.

Cakes and Candles

AFSC has helped a number of women's groups organize cooperative activities for income. A women's candle-making workshop was started in the town of Gabu, using locally available beeswax. AFSC provided the funds to build the two-room workshop and to purchase wicks, vats for melting the wax and a device for dipping the candles. The demand for candles is high because most villages have no electricity, and oil for lamps is scarce and expensive. The women can make about 200 candles an hour.

The first and only bakery in the region of Cacheu, the Canchungo Bakery, was funded and equipped by AFSC. A group of 23 women joined together to make bread and cakes to sell to the community. They constructed the building, using mud bricks they made themselves. "The women are interested in cultivating wheat so they can make their own flour, baking with manioc flour and trying other techniques. Their hope isn't to become rich, but to contribute more to the family income for expenses such as medicines and school supplies."

Two soap-making units have been set up by AFSC in two rural areas and a third is planned. AFSC imports the caustic soda; palm oil is available locally.

Grinding and Dehulling Machines

AFSC imported eight millet-grinding machines and distributed them to women's groups around Guinea-Bissau. "Millet—ground to various textures—is used to make bread, as a rice substitute, or for baby food," Nichols reports. "The grinding that used to take five hours by hand now takes 15 to 20 minutes by machine, making, for example, enough baby cereal for 7 to 10 days."

Rice is one of the hardest grains to clean. The AFSC has placed motor-driven rice dehulling machines in seven villages. This not only saves women hours of pounding by hand, but enables them to process additional rice for sale. Dehulled rice brings a much higher price and so greater income. People come by canoe from miles around to use the machines. One rice dehuller may serve as many as ten villages. "There has been an unbelievable response from both men and women," Nichols says. "The men are pleased because they now have more time with their wives who aren't nearly as tired at the end of the day. And the women have more time for their children."

With the time saved from pounding rice, women can participate in other activities, such as taking courses in literacy, bookkeeping, gardening, animal husbandry. One woman is raising chickens, another is studying health care so she can better care for her family. The AFSC plans to place seven more machines in other villages in the near future.

Zimbabwe Family-Planning Project

U.S. Agency for International Development

Zimbabwe has had a strong family-planning program for over 20 years. The Zimbabwe National Family Planning Council is the primary organization responsible for the delivery of family-planning services; it runs what is widely recognized as one of the most innovative and well-organized programs in Africa.

Shortly after Zimbabwe's independence in 1980, AID approved an $8.5 million project with the council. (The project has been extended, and the current completion date is 1990.) The purpose of the project is to assist the council to strengthen and expand family-planning services. The original proposal listed five objectives:

● strengthening the management of the Zimbabwe National Family Planning Council;

● reaching a larger number of families with the child-spacing service programs of the council and the Ministry of Health and increasing their geographic distribution;

● establishing a research and evaluation department within the council;

● improving the council's information, education and communications activities; and

● increasing and improving the systematic training of educators/distributors, medical assistants, youth advisers and group leaders. These remain the principal objectives of the project, although there is more emphasis on the council's working with the private sector.

On the basis of experience, the project expanded its aims:

Community-based distribution services in rural areas

Appropriate technology: A hand-operated corn mill (right) is more popular than a gas-driven mill (left) that often breaks down.

remain the primary outreach goal. The project currently supports the salaries of 360 workers, 68 group leaders and 3 additional senior educators in the largest provinces. It also provided for the purchase of 70 motorcycles and 510 bicycles for the use of educators/distributors and supervisors in rural areas; and equipment, contraceptive supplies, materials and training. Studies will be made of the cost effectiveness of the program and the possible use of supply depots at the village level.

The **youth advisory services** are being expanded, with the training of 30 new youth advisers. Support includes salary, travel and allowance, audio-visual equipment and educational materials. The council is extending the youth advisory services' outreach through workshops and training for youth leaders in other government ministries and institutions.

The **training programs** for Ministry of Health workers and new community-based distribution service workers and supervisors are being expanded, as is clinical family-planning training, including instruction in the insertion of intrauterine devices (IUDs). Observation study tours and short-term out-of-country training for 80 international participants are also being arranged.

While the council covers most of the costs of **medical/clinical services**, the project underwrites the salaries of two new physicians, four new nurses and laundry and cooking equipment. The project also provides supplies, such as IUD insertion and removal kits and blood pressure machines.

To improve its management and administration, AID provided the council with funds to hire an operations manager and a secretary and to finance an outside management audit to identify weaknesses and make recommendations to improve the program.

To strengthen **evaluation and research**, AID funded the hiring of a social science adviser for three years, three Zimbabwean social scientists and a statistician/programmer. It also provided for the purchase of seven microcomputers and long-term masters-level training in the United States for three social scientists.

Zimbabwe has a well-organized and large **private sector**, including commercial farms, mines, large industrial companies and commercial retail outlets, which provides a large percentage of the population with some form of health service. There are approximately 900 private-sector health facilities. Of these only 133, or 15 percent, received contraceptives from the council. The council plans to increase family-planning information and service delivery to these private-sector groups.

Either through the council or a local nongovernmental organization, the project will make funds available to develop small family-planning subprojects in collaboration with various private-sector groups. For industries or companies that primarily employ men, the focus will be on family-planning educational programs and condom distribution. For organizations where health services are provided to employees and their families, projects will introduce or expand family-planning information and services. A key feature of the program is to demonstrate to the private firms the cost-effectiveness and financial benefits of family planning. Initially the private-sector groups will receive assistance to introduce family planning, but eventually it is hoped they will purchase both contraceptive supplies and technical assistance from the council.

Unresolved Issues

The management structure of the Zimbabwe National Family Planning Council is still fragile, and a major disruption could undo much of the project's success. There is still confusion concerning lines of authority, job responsibility and equitable levels of pay. By and large the problems can only be solved by the council and its board. Additional funds will not substantially relieve these problems.

Whether the government of Zimbabwe will be willing and able to assume the costs of the program once the AID project ends is another concern. But since the government now covers 60 percent of the costs and can be expected to increase its revenue collection in the future, there is good reason to believe it will be able to carry the full costs of the project.

The cost of the program, 1982-90, will be $18,542,000.

Talking It Over

A Note for Students and Discussion Groups

This issue of the HEADLINE SERIES, like its predecessors, is published for every serious reader, specialized or not, who takes an interest in the subject. Many of our readers will be in classrooms, seminars or community discussion groups. Particularly with them in mind, we present below some discussion questions—suggested as a starting point only—and references for further reading.

Discussion Questions

How have decisions made at the Conference of Berlin over 100 years ago affected latter-day Africa?

What were some of the major legacies of the colonial period in Africa? How did colonialism affect living patterns and the continent's biological carrying systems?

One of the striking features of precolonial Africa was the genetic diversity of its plants and the variety of food produced. How has this changed? What implications do the changes have for Africa? for the North?

Africa has given to the world for centuries, the author writes, but the world has put little back. What does he mean by this statement?

Development strategists will probably have to base their future planning on shifts in the weather measured in geological time, according to the author. What evidence does he cite to substantiate this statement?

What are some of the signs of an impending famine? What early-warning systems, if any, are reliable?

What are some of the cultural factors that affect population growth in Africa? What are some of the author's recommendations for a population strategy in Africa?

Cite ways in which agricultural production could be increased.

What are some of the trends that inspire confidence in Africa's long-term future?

READING LIST

General Development Policy Issues

Africa Tomorrow. Report by the U.S. Office of Technology Assessment, December 1984. Washington, D.C., USGPO, 1984. Careful analysis of current modes of development by donor agencies; forward-looking but realistic.

Berg, Elliot, *Accelerated Development in Sub-Saharan Africa: An Agenda for Action*. Washington, D.C., The World Bank, 1981. Argues for shift in World Bank fiscal policies toward the South.

Brown, Lester, and Wolf, Edward C., "Reversing Africa's Decline," *Worldwatch Paper 65*, June 1985. Available from Worldwatch Institute, 1776 Massachusetts Avenue, N.W., Washington, D.C. 20036. Calls for a broadbased effort to restore and preserve Africa's natural support systems.

Bulletin of the Atomic Scientists, September 1985. Special section devoted to Africa, with articles on food, security, the military, agricultural research, drought, food aid, self-sufficiency.

Eagleburger, Lawrence S., and McHenry, Donald F., "Compact for African Development." Report of the Committee on African Development Strategies. New York and Washington, D.C., Council on Foreign Relations and Overseas Development Council, December 1985. Report argues for a strong, long-term commitment by Africa, the United States and other nations to help Africa help itself.

The Lagos Plan of Action for the Implementation of the Monrovia Strategy for the Economic Development of Africa. Organization of African Unity Report 1980. Geneva, Switzerland, International Labor Organization for the Organization of African Unity, 1981. African nations plan their own salvation.

Timberlake, Lloyd, *Africa in Crisis: The Causes, The Cures of Environmental Bankruptcy.* Washington, D.C., Earthscan, 1985. Award-winning analysis of problems in African environment, with special reference to development debate.

Williams, Albert L., *United States International Economic Policy in an Interdependent World.* Report to President Richard M. Nixon, 1971. Washington, D.C., USGPO, 1979. Key report by the U.S. Commission on International Trade and Investment which has determined U.S. foreign development policy since 1971.

Willis, David K., *Africa: Blueprint for Survival.* Boston, Mass., The Christian Science Monitor Reprints, 1985. Five-part series on African development issues.

Agriculture and Food Production

"Africa Emergency." Monthly update on the food crisis available from United Nations Office for Emergency Operations in Africa, 866 United Nations Plaza, New York, N.Y. 10017.

"Africa: the Potential for Higher Food Production." Special Report No. 125, U.S. Department of State, Bureau of Public Affairs, Washington, D.C. 20520. A brief, illustrated report on the agricultural crisis.

Chambers, Robert, *The Crisis of Africa's Rural Poor: Perceptions and Priorities.* Institute of Development Studies, University of Sussex, Brighton, Sussex BN 19RE, U.K., February 1985. Bottom-up approach to development through human resources.

George, Susan, *How the Other Half Dies: The Real Reasons for World Hunger.* Totowa, N.J., Allanheld, Osmun & Co., 1977. Closely and persuasively argued book outlining the failures of the dominant agriculture and high-tech models favored by large donor agencies.

Land, Food and People. Geneva, Switzerland, Food and Agriculture Organization, 1985. Analysis of balance in Africa between land, people and their food requirements.

Sen, Amartya, *Poverty and Famines: An Essay on Entitlement.* New York, Oxford University Press, 1981. Are people entitled to food as a basic human right?

Upton, Martin, *Farm Management in Africa.* New York, Oxford University Press, 1980. Practical analysis of farming today in Africa.

Health and Population Issues

Caldwell, John C., and Caldwell, Pat, *Cultural Forces Tending to Sustain High Fertility in Tropical Africa.* Canberra, Australia, Australian National University, 1984. Clearly argued private report on religion and cultural forces sustaining high population growth in Africa.

McNamara, Robert S., "Time Bomb or Myth: The Population Problem." *Foreign Affairs,* Summer 1984. Analysis of global population problem by former World Bank president.

The Primary Health Worker. Geneva, Switzerland, World Health Organization, 1977. Village-level health work following a basic-needs approach.

Shepherd, Gill, *Responding to the Contraception Needs of the Rural People: Kenya 1984.* Oxfam, 274 Banbury Rd., Oxford, U.K., 1984. Perceptive analysis of why family planning has not worked in Kenya and how to make it work.

Werner, David, *Where There Is No Doctor: A Village Health Care Handbook.* Palo Alto, Calif., The Hesperian Foundation, 1977. Outline of barefoot-doctor approach to health problems in the South.

Climate, Desertification and Development Issues

Cutler, Peter, "Famine Forecasting; Prices and Peasant Behavior in Northern Ethiopia." *Disasters: International Journal of Disaster Studies,* No. 8, January 1984. Available from International Disaster Institute, Foxcombe Publications, 13 Underhill Lane, Lower Burne, Farnham, Surry, U.K. A new, low-cost model for early warning of famine based on prices, movement of cattle, distribution of foodstuffs and other domestic phenomena.

Garcia, Rolando V., *Nature Pleads Not Guilty: An IFIAS Report*. Elmsford, N.Y., Pergamon, 1981. Volume 1 of academically elegant arguments exploding popular myths in respect to development, food aid, population and climate.

Grainger, Alan, *Desertification: How People Make Deserts, How People Can Stop, and Why They Don't*. Washington, D.C., Earthscan, 1983. Well-documented and illustrated assessment of global problem of expanding deserts.

Winstanley, Derek, "Africa in Drought: A Change of Climate?" *Weatherwise* No. 36, April 1985. Short article arguing from basis of diaries and reports of past 200 years that drought is a permanent trend in Sahelian zone of Africa.

HS 274, May/June 1985

Since 1918, the Foreign Policy Association has worked to help Americans gain a better understanding of problems in U.S. foreign policy and to stimulate informed citizen discussion of, and participation in, world affairs.

The Association is independent and nonpartisan, has no affiliation with government and takes no position on questions under debate. Rather, it seeks to call attention to, and to clarify opposing views on, those foreign policy issues which government and people must resolve in democratic partnership.

FPA's publications, in addition to the year-round HEADLINE *Series, include the annual* Great Decisions, *a briefing and discussion guide on eight current foreign policy topics. Reports on the annual* Great Decisions *"Opinion Ballots" are a valued index to the foreign policy views of informed citizens. Both directly and through the media support they receive, FPA publications reach out to more students, libraries, citizens and community groups than any other world affairs educational service today.*

FPA provides an open world affairs meeting service to the New York and Washington communities. Throughout the year, FPA's podium, with the opportunity of audience discussion, is offered to leaders, experts and institutions concerned with, and taking varying positions on, current issues of U.S. foreign policy.

By such means, FPA seeks to achieve what Elihu Root emphasized in the early years of the Association's existence:

"The control of foreign relations by modern democracies creates a new and pressing demand for popular education in international affairs."

Foreign Policy Association
Editorial Advisory Committee

FPA's Editorial Advisory Committee was formed to give the Association's publishing program the benefit of a wide range of talent in journalism, broadcasting, education, community service and business. Topics, approaches, authors, and audiences to be served by future FPA publications are discussed by the Committee and FPA's editors at their meetings.